AF573701

Mercian & Welsh Buses in Camera

MALCOLM KEELEY

LONDON

IAN ALLAN LTD

First published 1974

ISBN 0 7110 0516 8

Published by Ian Allan Ltd, Shepperton, Surrey and printed in the United Kingdom by Morrison & Gibb Ltd, London and Edinburgh

Contents

CHESTERFIELD
12
383 ENN

Introduction

THIS IS NOT JUST AN ALBUM of bus photographs, it is an attempt to reach pictorially the very heart of bus transport and discover why it provides a fascination for so many of us. Many, many different aspects knit together to form the rich tapestry that is the bus industry—your interest may be in vehicles, ancient and modern, chassis types, bodybuilders, running units, how they go and the sounds they make, routes, or simply the work of transport people. All are mentioned in the following pages.

This particular volume covers the slab of land from the top of Yorkshire and Lancashire down to the south Midlands—plus the whole of Wales and the Isle of Man. For convenience the title Mercian and Welsh Buses in Camera has been chosen and we trust that it will not offend those included not strictly covered by the territory suggested in the title. Excluded are the undertakings that were merged to form passenger transport authorities in 1969—they have been treated in a separate volume.

Each chapter studies buses in different surroundings and hopefully will also reveal the human side—transport is provided by people for people. Regard is paid to some of today's problems but this is not a book for those who merely study transport as part of the job, it is for those who are genuinely interested in buses themselves and their operation—those who like to escape back into the past now and again and say "Ah! Yes!" By taking the work of some of the country's best bus photographers, each with his own particular brand of photography, I hope to have captured as many of the different aspects as possible. Naturally space has proved a crippling factor so a time limit has been set, you will find no pictures taken before 1930 if only because so many of today's enthusiasts are unable to identify with the vehicles built before then. Instead I have concentrated on the varied vehicles operated in the thirties and forties and even the fifties which, assisted by the Government's bus grant scheme, are now rapidly disappearing from the streets. Later types are also reviewed but less thoroughly as they are still with us and reflect increasing strides towards uniformity. Thus there is plenty of scope for wallowing in nostalgia, not only for past vehicles but for fleets and liveries which are no longer with us.

February 1973 M.R.K.

Left: An AEC Reliance/Weymann of East Midland finds a peaceful spot when new in 1960

War of the Roses—
Transport Style.

A Lancaster 1939 Daimler COG5/Willowbrook stands in the bus station during June, 1954

Lancashire quality. The Leyland double-deck body in its final form—a classic in British bus design. This PD2/10, built the year before Leyland ceased bodybuilding in 1954, was further enhanced by Darwen Corporation's bold lining-out in June, 1957. Cobbles and the market complete this picture of Darwen's Town Hall Square

Two unusual Yorkshiremen in the Yorkshire Traction fleet. The Dennis Lancet on the left makes a change from the Leyland Tiger that usually carried this style of BET Federation bodywork, in this case built by Brush in 1950. A Windover-bodied Royal Tiger coach, a year younger, stands to the right in August, 1961

1 Newcomers

How many readers' interest in transport was first aroused by the sight of a new bus? With some the fascination seems to be born within. With others, a boy's natural curiosity for discovering how things work or where they go may eventually lead him around to buses especially if there is something new to catch his eye. He might not like what he sees but nevertheless it registers and his interest is kindled.

A new bus is rather special even if it is of a type that has been seen before. It will never look quite as immaculate again, not even after a major overhaul—nothing recaptures that crisp "newness", except perhaps on the most expensively preserved specimens. It is not surprising the garage engineer jealously guards his latest delivery like a new-born babe, particularly if it is the first of a new design. A driver will be threatened with a fate worse than death if he dares to put even so much as a half-inch scratch on it. Of course, apparently unknown to the garage engineer, the driver is just as anxious not to soil the newcomer although one day, life being the way it is, the new bus will come back "desecrated" in some way. Its virginity thus lost, both engineer and driver can then relax and treat it like any other.

The officials seem pleased with the angle of tilt attained by their Daimler CVG6—note the ropes are still slack. ANH 153 was a new Northern Coachbuilders-bodied bus for Northampton Corporation in June, 1947

Ordinary passengers are a little slower on the uptake. A vehicle has to be remarkably different in layout before many will notice anything new. In towns where rear-loaders were legion the arrival of the first front-entrance buses did manage to excite some comment. Once aboard however amnesia would set in, particularly upstairs, and on every journey there would always be somebody making his way to the back to alight despite the tide of departing passengers coming the other way. It only turned really nasty when drunks and other late night revellers would try to get ON at the back. Change however is usually very gradual but one day the passenger may look around him and perhaps appreciate that the vehicle he is travelling in really is much better equipped than the one fifteen years ago.

From the operator's viewpoint there is always some advantage to a new vehicle whether it be for larger capacity, one-manning, a new type of service or just because the existing fleet is wearing out and not worth overhauling. Once upon a time the operator had to balance the savings to be obtained with new buses against the cost of purchasing them. Now with high labour costs v the Government's generous bus grant, the choice is becoming easier.

1949

A rear-entrance Regal III/ Weymann, destined to become hopelessly out-of-date within a year, leaves the AEC factory for East Midland. Meanwhile Midland Red had well and truly beaten the manufacturers to the post by producing its own reliable underfloor-engined models in quantity since 1946.

1949
An S9 receives a body to Midland Red design at the Brush works in Loughborough

The prewar Burton Corporation fleet consisted almost entirely of Guy single-deckers. This 1934 BB-type with Gardner 4LW engine and Guy body was amongst its first oilers

Longwell Green bus bodies are becoming increasingly rare, the last to be built were a pair on AEC Regent V chassis for Pontypridd UDC. No93 enjoys a quite moment in Caerphilly bus station when new in 1966—note the 'vintage' fleet numbers

One of Rotherham's first delivery of Crossleys, **186** looked particularly smart in its original livery when photographed on Effingham Street during May, 1949. **The** fascinating machine behind is one of Rotherham's single-ended tramcars withdrawn the same year

As good as new! Manufacturers' demonstrators give operators the chance to evaluate new models—this SMC (Sunbeam) Sikh, later acquired by Derby Corporation, is seen in **Mansfield District livery**

A former Earls Court exhibit in West Riding colours is this Wakefield-registered AEC Regal IV/Roe seen soon after with T. Williams & Sons, Ponciau

Replacements for the trolleybuses to Parr stand in St Helens depot in December 1955. Yet to carry passengers, the Leyland Titan PD2/20s bear East Lancs bodies painted in the Corporation's attractive red and cream

An immaculate petrol Leyland Tiger TS7 of United Counties at Southgate Street, Leicester in August, 1935. The coach bodywork incorporating roof luggage rack was by Eastern Counties

Two Roe-bodied Daimler Fleetlines working in Huddersfield. Note that the opportunity to use a wrap-round screen was not taken on the double-decker.
St George's Square in 1969

A pleasant suburban scene in Nottingham showing a new Brush-bodied Ransomes trolleybus in 1932. This generation of trolleys looked wider at the top than the bottom

Proud of its air-suspension was this ex-demonstration AEC Bridgemaster snapped up by Barton Transport. Its Crossley body was of much better proportions than the austere Park Royals fitted to the production Bridgemasters. 805 at Beeston Square

Similarly advertising itself was United Counties' first FS6B-type Bristol Lodekka at Northampton bus station in 1960

Peak period traffic in Broadgate, Coventry in 1969. In the foreground are Fleetlines bodied by Willowbrook, East Lancs and ECW. Behind are Metro-Cammell Orion-bodied Daimler CVG6s and a Leyland Atlantean/ Willowbrook. Also conspicuous in the picture are five cars carrying only six passengers and taking up the space of at least two Fleetlines

2 Into the Fray

SMALL WONDER THAT THOSE RESPONSIBLE for a new bus wait in trepidation for its return after the first day in service. Driving a car in peak-period conditions like those seen on the left can be worrying enough—but imagine handling a new 12-metre job which can be guaranteed to reveal some odd characteristics not discovered on familiarisation runs. However the professional driver soon gets the hang of any new type that comes his way, and in next to no time the more spirited will no doubt be hurling their steeds round the city centre just like the old 'uns. Developments in gearbox and cab design plus increased efficiency in other units have made the driver's life much easier. Watch the driver of a Leyland National and see how every control has been placed within easy reach.

For years, more and more money has been poured into building roads designed to eliminate traffic congestion. Unfortunately far from alleviating trouble the "improvements" have generated even more traffic until the benefits can no longer be seen. At long last however the city planners are turning against the car. Besides parking restrictions which have been steadily mounting over the years there is now the pedestrianisation of once-busy streets in an ever growing number of towns. Whilst this is

Anyone for Skeggy? The author wouldn't have minded joining the passengers on a warm day in May, 1955 when Barton was still using double-deckers on its Nottingham–Skegness service. The bus is one of its long-lived fleet of distinctive Leyland PD1/Duple 55 seaters delivered in 1947–8, a rare combination of lowbridge construction and front-entrance. The latter caused their main drawback for long-distance services—poor visibility for the lower saloon passengers

hardly of any direct help to the bus, it is still extra discouragement to the private motorist. Even better news is the decision of Nottingham Corporation to scrap its roadbuilding programme with all the added environmental problems, and instead back its public transport system with increased frequencies and bus priority lanes. Everybody who fears the social consequences of destroying cities for the benefit of the private car will join bus enthusiasts in hoping Nottingham's courageous experiment succeeds, and also hope that other towns will soon follow suit.

Buses fortunately do not spend all day tangled in traffic jams and photographs in this chapter will reveal that there are periods of running that can almost be described as restful. The territory of this book of course includes areas that are distinctly rural in nature and there the services are not only *too* restful but downright unprofitable. There are also glances at transport operation in wartime; spare a thought for those overworked crews and overloaded buses, and in particular those drivers who at night, deprived of street lighting, depended on masked lamps and moonlight for their progress.

A 1945 Bristol K6A of Aberdare UDC loads in the main street in September, 1952. The earliest Bristols constructed after production was resumed towards the end of 1944 had the high radiators associated with prewar models. Park Royal utility bodywork was fitted

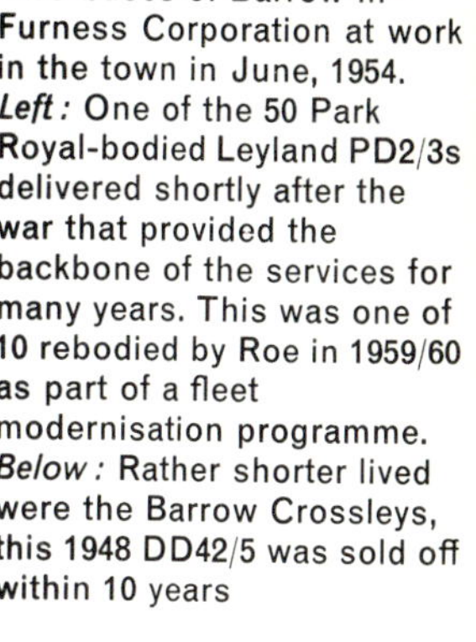

Two buses of Barrow-in-Furness Corporation at work in the town in June, 1954. *Left:* One of the 50 Park Royal-bodied Leyland PD2/3s delivered shortly after the war that provided the backbone of the services for many years. This was one of 10 rebodied by Roe in 1959/60 as part of a fleet modernisation programme. *Below:* Rather shorter lived were the Barrow Crossleys, this 1948 DD42/5 was sold off within 10 years

Never mind the quality, feel the width! The burned-out shell of the YMCA buildings in Forster Square, Bradford provides a grim background to Corporation trolley 694 in 1952. Ten of these 8ft wide Sunbeam chassis were destined for Johannesburg in 1942 but diverted to Bradford and fitted with these Weymann utility bodies—8ft wide buses were not normally permitted in this country until 1946

Burton-upon-Trent is a brewery town and you know it as soon as you step off the train. A Corporation Guy Arab III loads in the busy road opposite the station in March, 1961 whilst a Bedford van works wonders in the opposite direction. The bus carried lowbridge Roberts bodywork and dated from 1947

The low winter sunshine in late 1939 catches the windscreen of new Blackburn Corporation Regent/East Lancs 55 bound for Accrington whilst a TD5 makes its way in the background. Life goes on as normally as possible in that first nervous winter of the war—how popular hats were then!

The Blue Bus, of Willington, Daimler CD650s are well known but not so some of their predecessors from the same stable. A 1948 CVD6 with heavily-rebuilt Strachans bodywork takes the island near Derby bus station in September, 1962 closely pursued by a Trent AEC Regent II/Willowbrook, once ubiquitous throughout Trent's territory

The sun creeps out after a summer shower in August, 1952. A Burnley, Colne & Nelson Leyland Titan TD5 bodied by East Lancs samples the freshened air

Typically Blackpool Corporation in its unconventional appearance, this centre-entrance full-front Leyland Titan TD4 was meant to look streamlined. The body was built locally by Burlingham

6
FBE 742

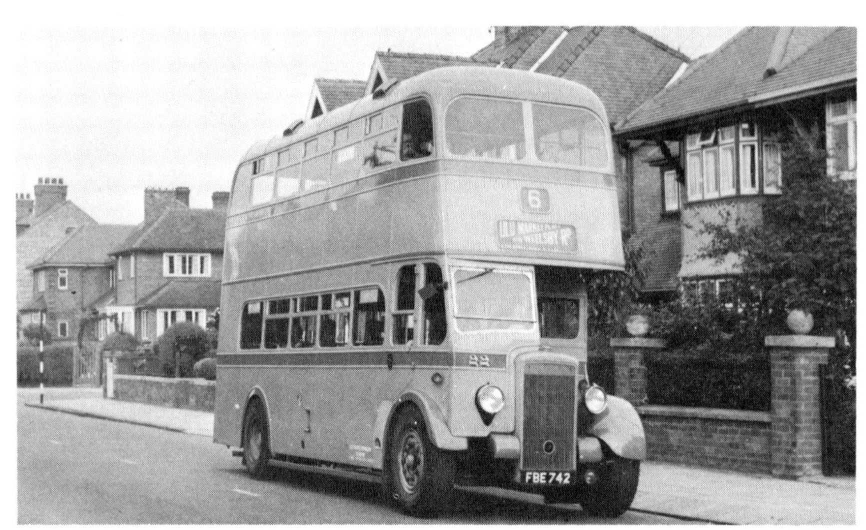

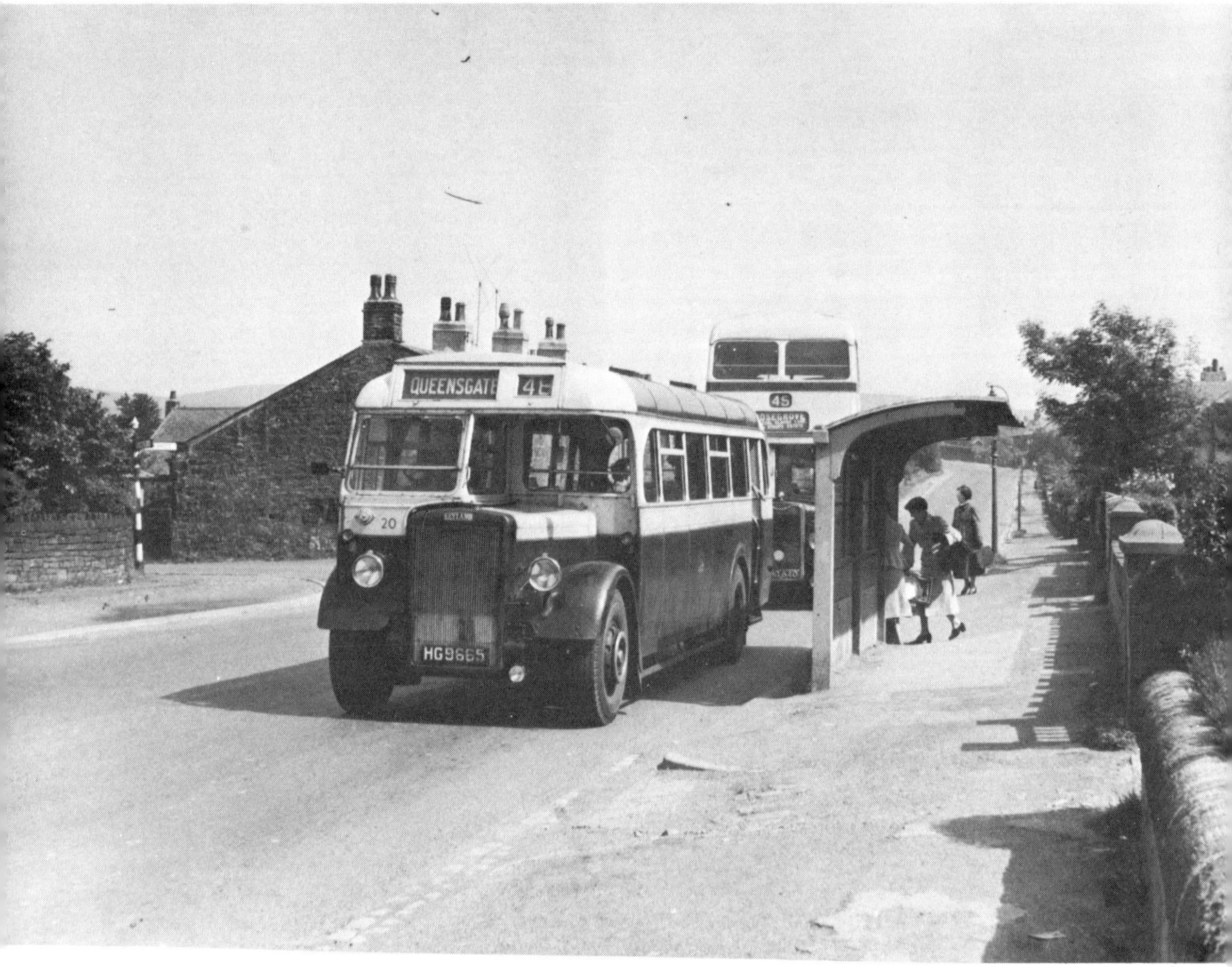
QUEENSGATE
4E
20
HG9665
45

Opposite, top: A Cleethorpes Corporation 1948 Willowbrook-bodied Daimler CVD6 seen working in the mid-fifties before the merger with Grimsby

Opposite, below: The north-east Lancashire towns are separated by delightful low hills seemingly always visible in the background. On the outskirts of Burnley in 1956 were these two Burnley, Colne & Nelson buses, a 1948 Massey-bodied Leyland Tiger PS1 bound for Queensgate garage and a 1951 Guy Arab IV/ East Lancs destinated for Rosegrove

The beautiful ancient city of Chester in the early months of 1940. Two Corporation buses are seen loading up, a 1939 Massey-bodied Regent complete with wartime headlamp masks leads

Despite the terrific beating it took, at least part of Coventry was still intact after the war. This very early postwar scene shows a Corporation Daimler COA6, the standard bus of the 1935–9 period. The COA6 was unique to Coventry, this 1935 example carried Metro-Cammell bodywork

Derby Corporation is not particularly associated with Leylands. A 'gearless' Brush-bodied Tiger turns out of Victoria Street into the Cornmarket in September, 1936

Accrington's buses were an unusual combination of dark blue and red with black window surrounds. The smart appearance of this 1951 all-Leyland PD2/3 in September, 1962 was finished off by gold lining-out. Window surrounds are now also painted a dark blue

Very much history is this October, 1962 picture of the Bamber Bridge Motor Services AEC Regent III/East Lancs in Preston. BBMS was taken over by Ribble in 1967 whilst the area on which the immaculate No4 stood has since been redeveloped

The traditional City of Oxford Motor Services livery is unfortunately now out of favour. About to cross over Magdalen Bridge and the River Cherwell into High Street, 325 passes through The Plain in May, 1971; these short-length front-entrance AEC Bridgemasters were exclusive to Oxford

Narrow streets in the centre of Heptonstall are brightened by the green, orange and cream Halifax buses. A dog finds this Joint Committee Roe-bodied AEC Regal III of particular interest in May, 1963

A newly overhauled bus is always a fine sight, especially when carrying a bright new livery like this Nottingham Corporation PD2/Metro-Cammell in October, 1962. Shortly afterwards the livery was again modified, vehicles being painted with green upper deck window surrounds

Also in Nottingham is the independent South Notts Bus Co. with its curious blue, maroon and cream livery. A lowbridge 1961 Leyland PD3/Northern Counties leaves the old Broadmarsh bus station for the giant Clifton estate in 1970

Two of East Yorkshire's unusual Gothic roof double-deckers in Hull in October, 1962. Note the cream wheels and how the very top of the roof and all the rear dome is painted blue. On the left is a full-fronted 1951 PD2/Roe (a 'Bluebottle') whilst alongside is a Roe-bodied PD1, one of many supplied just after the war

A Lancashire hotpot. This veteran 1934 English Electric-bodied Leyland Titan TD3 of Southport basks in the hot sunshine on Ainsdale beach in June, 1963

Two busy scenes in Derby. Above a 1936 Guy BTX/Brush takes on a heavy load near the bus station in the early fifties whilst below a Sunbeam/Brush leads another Sunbeam, a 1960 Roe-bodied F4A, through the Market Place. Daimler buses also with Brush and Roe bodywork bring up the rear. Note the different livery applied to motorbuses

Coaching pre-war style. A Saturday afternoon scene in Huntingdon Street bus station with three Leylands heading homewards to Yorkshire. A Yorkshire Woollen Duple-bodied Tiger is flanked by Roe- and Brush-bodied examples of East Yorkshire

The arrival of underfloor-engined chassis allowed coach designers to give full rein to their imaginations. A number of bizarre shapes was concocted, many evidently deriving inspiration from American cars of the period. Hardly restrained, but not unattractive, were the four Bellhouse-Hartwell bodied Leyland Royal Tigers supplied to Hebble in 1954. No36 leaves Dewsbury bus station in July nine years later

Another evocative wartime scene as a 1937 AEC Regent/ Roe of Doncaster Corporation bound for Intake passes St Sepulchre Gate in the centre of the town

A pity no colour pictures have proved obtainable of East Midlands' old brown, yellow and cream livery. A new Leyland Titan TD4 with Leyland's first style of metal-frame body leaves Mansfield for Sheffield in May, 1935

A piano-front style AEC Regent of Hull Corporation years before the introduction of its famous livery of swoops and curves, itself now displaced

Grimsby Corporation standardised on centre-entrance Roe bodies for some years before the war including several trolleybuses on AEC chassis like No17 still working in the mid-fifties

There is a long-standing tradition of exhibiting a Roe-bodied vehicle for Leeds at the Commercial Motor Show. This AEC Swift was the 1966 exhibit and is seen later on a Fastaway limited stop service

Amongst the first and best of the so-called new look front end designs was the Foden. However the modern front often seemed an excuse to choose uninspiring bodywork—for instance this Welsh Metal Industries example of Merthyr Tydfil Corporation dating from 1948 and seen a year later

More in Merthyr's line in 1948 was the Bristol, this K6G had D. J. Davies bodywork later heavily rebuilt. The K6G itself was a rare model and was not generally supplied to the Tilling companies, Bristol's main customers

The heyday of Midland Red. An immaculate 1932 SOS REDD-type double-decker stands proudly at Dudley in August, 1938

Midland Red was allocated a number of unfrozen buses in 1942 which joined a fleet entirely of its own manufacture. The six Brush-bodied AEC Regents originally built for Coventry were however not completely unfamiliar as the earliest diesel SOS buses had AEC engines. 2441 leads two Birmingham City Transport COG5s at Five Ways, Birmingham when new

Still sadly missed by Midland Red drivers and enthusiasts alike are the 100 Leyland Titan PD2s with Leyland's own bodywork supplied in 1952–3. The front end design was intended to resemble Midland Red's own productions, Classified LD8 by Midland Red, 4018 pulls away in Hermitage Road, Solihull, when new

Somebody at Leyland must have liked the design as it was adopted as its standard new-look front end throughout the rest of the fifties. A 1958 Scout Titan PD3 with Burlingham bodywork is seen when new in Preston

A fine selection of Northampton Corporation Daimlers in June, 1959. From left to right a 1950 CVG6, a 1945 CWD6, a 1939 COG5, and a 1953 CVG6. Roe built the bodywork on all but the Duple-bodied CWD6

Northampton broke away from the Daimler tradition in 1946 with ten of these Crossley DD42/3s. More predictably Roe built the bodywork—a quarter of a century elapsed before any more non-Daimlers entered the fleet. 145 in the fifties

Comparatively deep windows on this prewar Mansfield District AEC Regent seen in May, 1952 contrast with the typically narrow Weymann windscreen

An empty street in Nottingham in March, 1934. Empty save for this Davidson-bodied Leyland Lion LT1 of Midland General which was once a demonstrator

Not surprisingly nearly all wartime Guys had bodies to austerity specification. However a handful of the earliest Mark Is received bodies of prewar design like the unfamiliar but attractive combination seen here. Midland General 190 with Weymann bodywork bearing a resemblance to prewar Liverpool AECs plods past a Trent Regent II/Willowbrook in Sutton Road, Mansfield in May, 1953

Left: A prewar picture of Preston—streets, buildings and buses all have a neat, spick and span appearance. Two Corporation gearless TD4c's with English Electric bodywork pass Miller Arcade and the billiard hall
Right: A grim early postwar scene reflecting years of shortage. Bradford Town Hall, since cleaned, dwarfs a prewar Karrier loading for Clayton in March, 1950. The Weymann body was replaced two years later by a new Crossley unit—first stage of an enlightened trolleybus modernisation and expansion programme by the new manager, Chaceley Humpidge

The war brought many unlikely combinations into many fleets. This Guy Arab with MCW body to Manchester pattern was an unusual addition to the Newport Corporation fleet. High Street was a bad spot for traffic in July, 1949

High Street, Huddersfield in wartime. A snout-fronted 1937 AEC Regent with Gardner 6LW engine and Brush bodywork passes 1934 Regal/Brush No12

This 1949 Bristol K5G of Pontypridd UDC carried Beadle bodywork of positively prewar appearance. 57 picks its way through traffic in the centre of Pontypridd in May, 1967

Jones the bus. The first Leyland Olympian to be built found its way into the fleet of Jones, Aberbeeg, in South Wales after a period as a demonstrator. The 1953 bus leaving Aberbeeg in May, 1965

The Treforest trading estate was opened to ease unemployment in the late 1930s and brought a lot of extra business to Pontypridd UDC. 1939 Bristol K5G 28 with Bristol bodywork awaits the expected passenger traffic in May, 1956

Also coping with the peak exodus in May, 1956 was this wartime Guy of Rhondda. The Beadle body was not the original

St Helens Corporation's replicas of the London RT will be familiar to many, but this one is slightly different. The upper deck, including the destination layout, was rebuilt by East Lancs to this style after a low bridge accident. No62 in September, 1959

A Daimler Freeline of Reliance Motor Services (E. Sherriff), Sutton-on-the-Forest on its old-established York–Helmsley service. JDN 712 is ably driven through York by Miss Sherriff in July, 1963

The photographer evidently provides greater interest than the surrounding architecture to the passengers of this 1946 6LW-engined Guy Arab II of Warrington Corporation. Weymann-bodied No13 in July, 1962

An early AEC Regent of South Wales Transport loads in the main street of Swansea in the thirties

A blending of styles in Bacup Road, Rawtenstall in July, 1972 as modern buildings seen the world over contrast with traditional Lancashire. The Rossendale bus reflects contrasting styles too—modern East Lancs front-entrance bodywork on Leyland PD3 chassis with classic exposed radiator—a solid, straightforward and reliable vehicle of 1966

South Wales Transport remained faithful to the Regent, here a Mk V passes a Guy Arab IV/Massey of Rees & Williams, Tycroes, in Swansea in July, 1968

Two Rotherham single-deck trolleys in April, 1948. A 1939 AEC 664T is followed by a 1942 Sunbeam MS2, East Lancs built the centre-entrance bodies. The AEC is on the Maltby service, reputed to have been the fastest trolleybus route in Britain

Another duo. Two Trent front-entrance Weymann-bodied AECs of 1937 in Mansfield Road, Nottingham —most of these Regents were rebodied after the war. Note the blacked-out 'keep left' bollard in this March, 1940, view

The revolutionary Guy Wulfrunian was designed in conjunction with West Riding which acquired either directly or indirectly most of those built. Since its inception, the model has had a rather unfortunate history and is already almost a memory. Attractively painted West Riding 1012, built in 1965, edges through traffic in Union Street, Wakefield, in July, 1971—note the angle of the front wheels

One of five 1957 Leyland PD2/20s with ECW bodies operated by Sheffield—for years ECW bodywork was restricted to nationalised undertakings and this rare combination was only made possible by the BTC participation in the B and C fleets. Building construction takes place behind 1292 near the railway station in July, 1971

Despite the large influx of new vehicles after the war, Wigan Corporation could still produce the occasional gem in August, 1953. 17A heads for Worsley Mesnes in the south of the town—the suffix letter indicates that the 1933 Leyland Tiger was already on borrowed time, having been 'replaced' by new PD2 17

Western Welsh acquired a fleet of small Albion Nimbuses for rural services at the turn of the sixties. No23 with Harrington 30-seat body is seen in picturesque Brecon when new in September, 1960

The immaculate seaside resort of Southport has equally smart buses. The corporation's first new-look front bus is seen in Eastbank Street Square in July, 1964, the ten-year-old PD2/20 with Weymann body hardly looked dated at the time

Wigan Corporation still retains its smart and distinctive crimson and white livery. The Northern Counties body on this 1961 Leyland PD3A/2 bears a resemblance to Southdown practice with its four-and-a-half bay construction but of course lacks the full width cab. No54 at Standish in June, 1965

GUJ 356

3 Together We Can Really Go Places

THE NATIONAL BUS COMPANY'S first big publicity campaign in 1972 included the above slogan. Service cuts over the last twenty years have made it more difficult "to go places" but at last the passenger transport industry is fighting the decline and fighting hard. Although ground has been lost in the stage carriage field, coach operations have gone on from strength to strength. Express inter-city services continue to do well even where they meet direct competition from British Rail's electrified lines. The latter are undeniably faster but coach travel still holds the advantage of cheapness. The NBC is to closely study and improve its express network —an overhaul which in all too many cases is long overdue.

But it is in the field of excursion and tours where the advances have really been made in recent years. With the introduction of motorways and faster vehicles the coach proprietor has been able to expand his programme of day excursions quite considerably. Although tempting sunspots abroad have taken business away from some of our traditional seaside centres,the enterprising coachman has had no difficulty in more than counteracting this with new inland attractions like wild-life parks. Some operators have a long and successful history of extended tours, and these have been joined

The remarkably durable Bedford OB is still to be found in the hands of independent operators linking rural communities. An OB/Duple ex-Gittins of Crickheath, here with Mid-Wales Motorways, Newtown, heaves its way to Cross Lanes from Welshpool on a market day service in August, 1971

Anyone failing to guess this location should be sentenced to a lifetime on the Big Dipper! Leyland PD3A/1 391 makes its way amidst the Blackpool illuminations in September, 1972. The Metro-Cammell bodywork on this batch reintroduced half cabs to the corporation fleet after many, many years

by shorter two or three day tours without adverse effect. In addition private hire is booming as never before. Needless to say the NBC is looking increasingly to this side of the business to help itself out of trouble, and whereas the above is mainly designed to cater for local markets, the NBC being nationwide is probably better placed to deal with the ever-increasing tourist traffic from abroad.

What about stage carriage? Some companies like Midland Red have offered day-anywhere tickets for years with varying degrees of success. Many places of minority interest can therefore be reached easily for a guaranteed cost without the worries of parking and only the shortcomings of infrequent services. They will have obvious attractions for the growing tourist market who increasingly go for the obscure rather than the traditional. Under the auspices of the NBC we can expect the introduction of a nationwide period traveller ticket available on both buses and railways. This may be the thinking behind the standardisation of liveries within the NBC so that a foreign tourist can pick out an NBC bus with ease—although a motif on the front would probably have done the job just as well without the, to some minds, psychologically bad manoeuvre of denying companies their individuality.

An AEC Regent/Metro-Cammell of Cardiff Corporation at the Duke Street/Kingsway crossing near Cardiff Castle in 1936. Note the position of the route number box—what a contrast with the vehicles on the joint Cardiff–Newport service today

The crooked spire is a famous, if initially alarming, sight for visitors to Chesterfield. A Corporation Weymann-bodied Leyland PD2/30 speeds past a tourist's A30 when new in **1958**

Clarence Bridge over the River Taff in Cardiff provides the distinctive background to this Corporation Bruce-bodied BUT trolley built with front-exit and rear-entrance for pay-as-you-enter operation. Like its brothers, **248** had been rebuilt to single entrance/exit by the time this picture was taken in October, **1964**

Delightful prewar scene in Lincoln with a Corporation all-Leyland Titan TD5 passing through the Stonebow in June, 1938. This is now a pedestrian way

A Sentinel of Morrison, of Tenby, in its home town in September, 1954. Morrison was subsequently taken over by Silcox, of Pembroke Dock

Chester Corporation buses cross the picturesque River Dee in 1957

Red & White Bristol RELL6G/ECW R665 is one of several in the blue and cream livery of Jones, Aberbeeg, in 1972. An MW is just visible in the hills behind the RELL

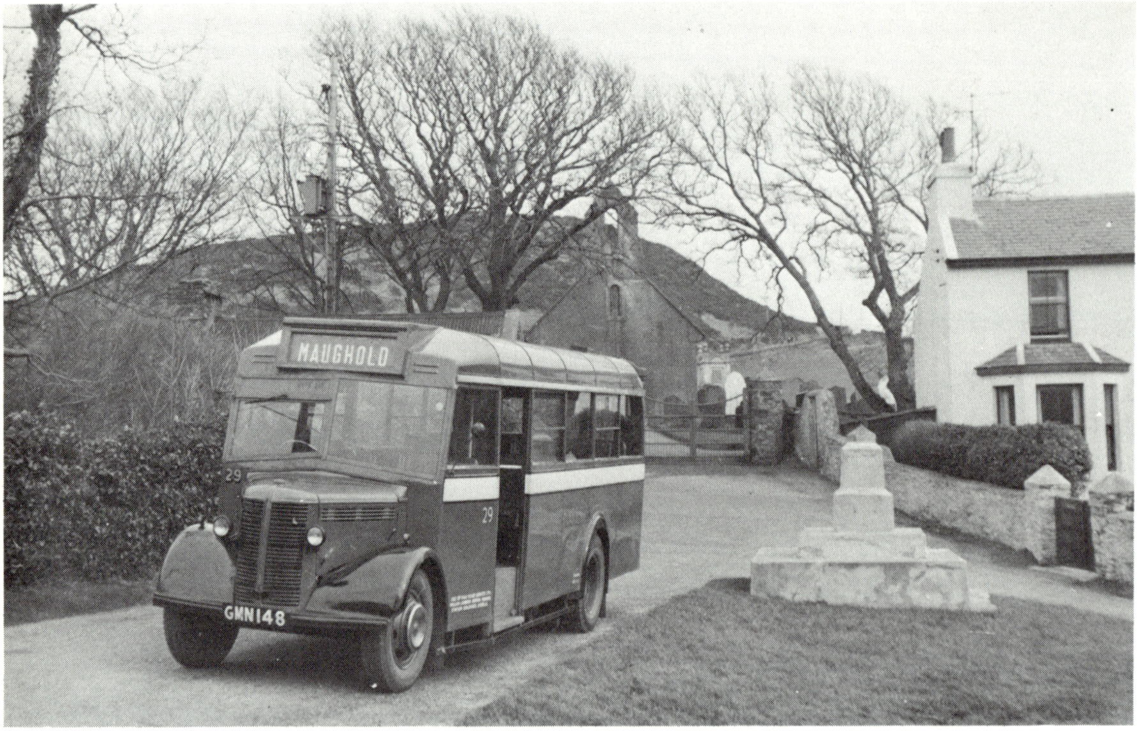

MAUGHOLD
29
GMN148

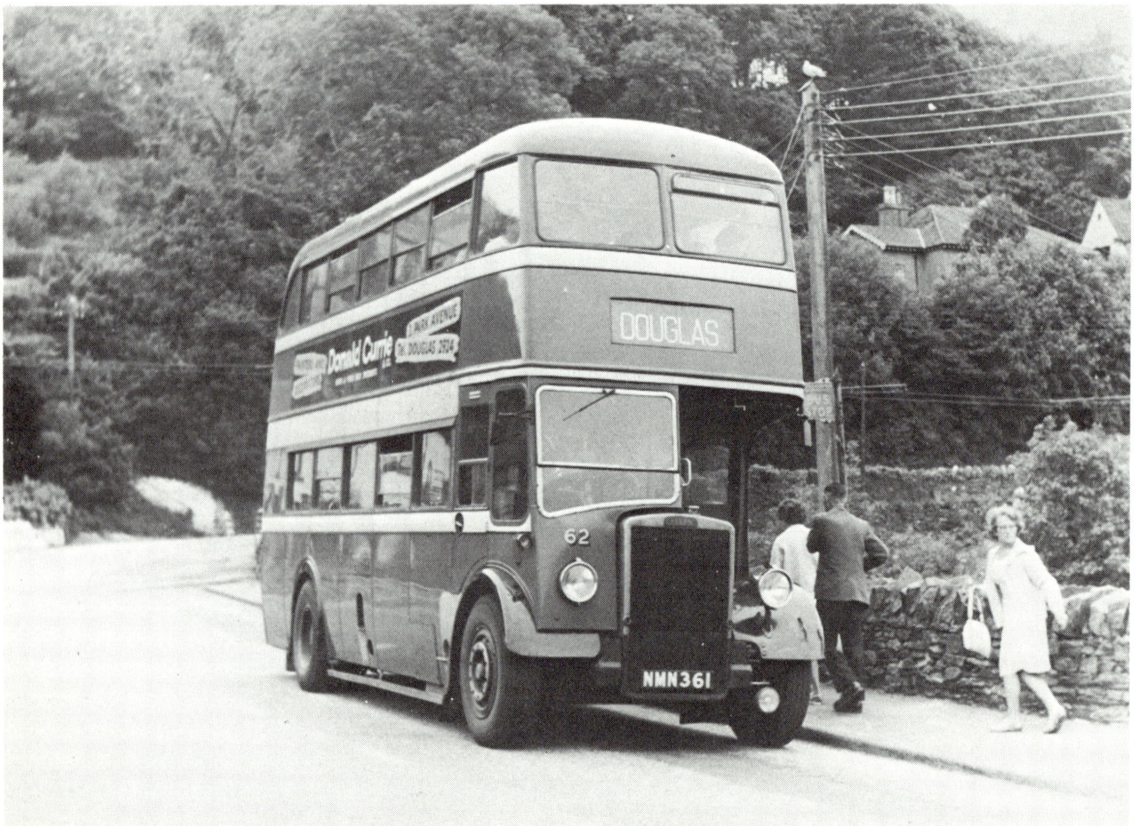

DOUGLAS
Donald Currie
62
NMN361

Opposite, top: Visitors to the Isle of Man for summer holidays will not associate the island with frosty mornings and leafless trees. A Road Services Bedford OWB pauses by the Cross at Maughold, near Ramsey, in March, 1967, shortly before its withdrawal

Opposite, below: ' 'Urry up, Maud, 'e's goin'.' Holiday-makers from cities on the mainland needlessly rush for the bus on this leisurely isle. A 1951 Road Services all-Leyland PD2/1, since rebuilt with sliding vents, waits near the Manx Electric Railway crossing at Laxey in July, 1965

Narrow streets are a feature of many older towns. Red & White MW U.859 threads its way through Abertillery in 1972

See the countryside by bus—preferably a double-decker. Upper deck passengers get an excellent view of Halkyn Church and the Dee estuary as the bus climbs towards Rhosesmor on Phillips' Holywell–Mold service in June, 1966. The 1956 PD2 carried a 1949 Burlingham body removed from a TD4c by the vehicle's original owner, Wallasey Corporation

Pembrokeshire is the favourite Welsh county for many people; Silcox, of Pembroke Dock, is the favourite fleet for many Bristol fans. The independent revealed a keen liking for Bristols in the years just after the war until their subsequent non-availability. This K6G seen in Pembroke Dock during September, 1954 carried Barnard lowbridge bodywork

Another Bristol, this time a K6B of Keighley-West Yorkshire carrying the particularly attractive ECW body of the early postwar period. All roads lead to KDB.35 as it bounces over the cobblestones amidst sooty buildings in Keighley during July, 1965

Coach excursions to beauty spots continue to give pleasure to young and old alike, and much-needed revenue to bus operators. One of Ribble's famous fleet of Leyland-bodied Royal Tigers, then considered revolutionary, made an early visit to Matlock Bath in May, 1951. Note the front seats are still occupied—presumably the passengers were not prepared to risk losing their excellent position previously only enjoyed by the engine

Typical of sixties' single-deckers is this 36ft AEC Reliance of Thomas Bros. seen against a background of hills in Port Talbot during April, 1968. History has already overtaken the photograph however; when the BET sold its bus interests to the state, the Thomas Bros. fleet disappeared in the National Bus Company's South Wales reorganisation

A Sheffield United Tours AEC Reliance/Plaxton passes through tourist-conscious Buxton in 1972

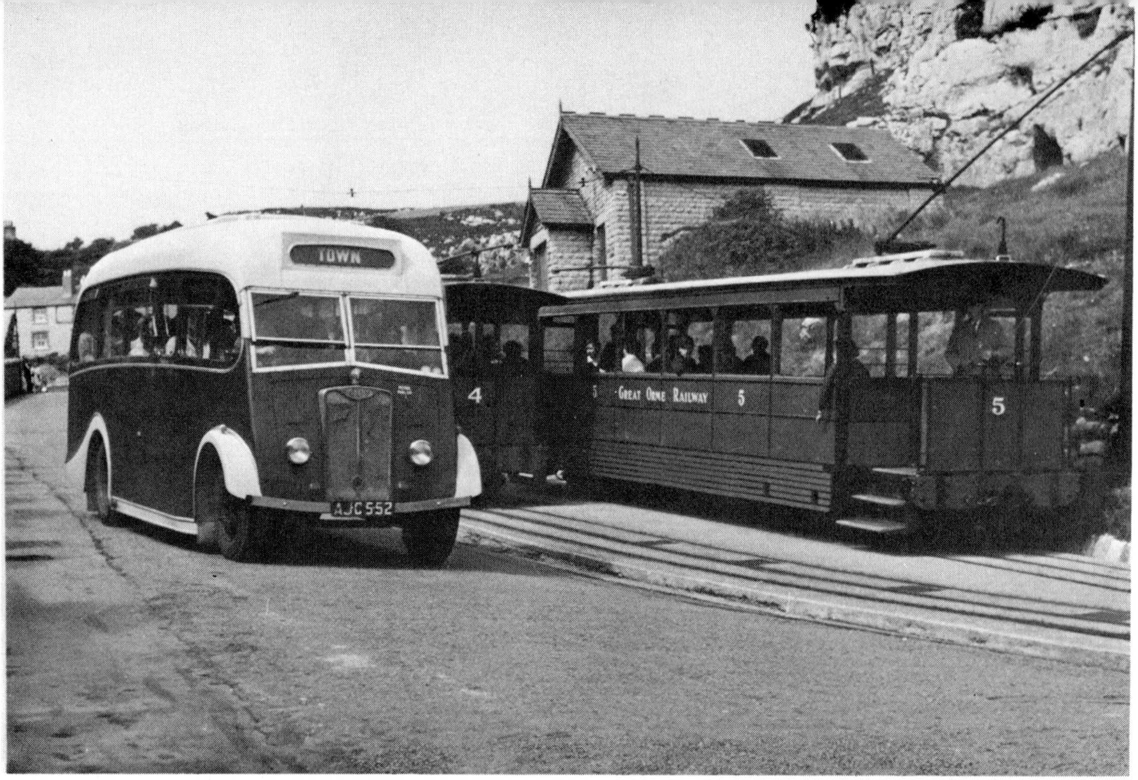
TOWN
AJC 552
4
GREAT ORME RAILWAY
5
5
5

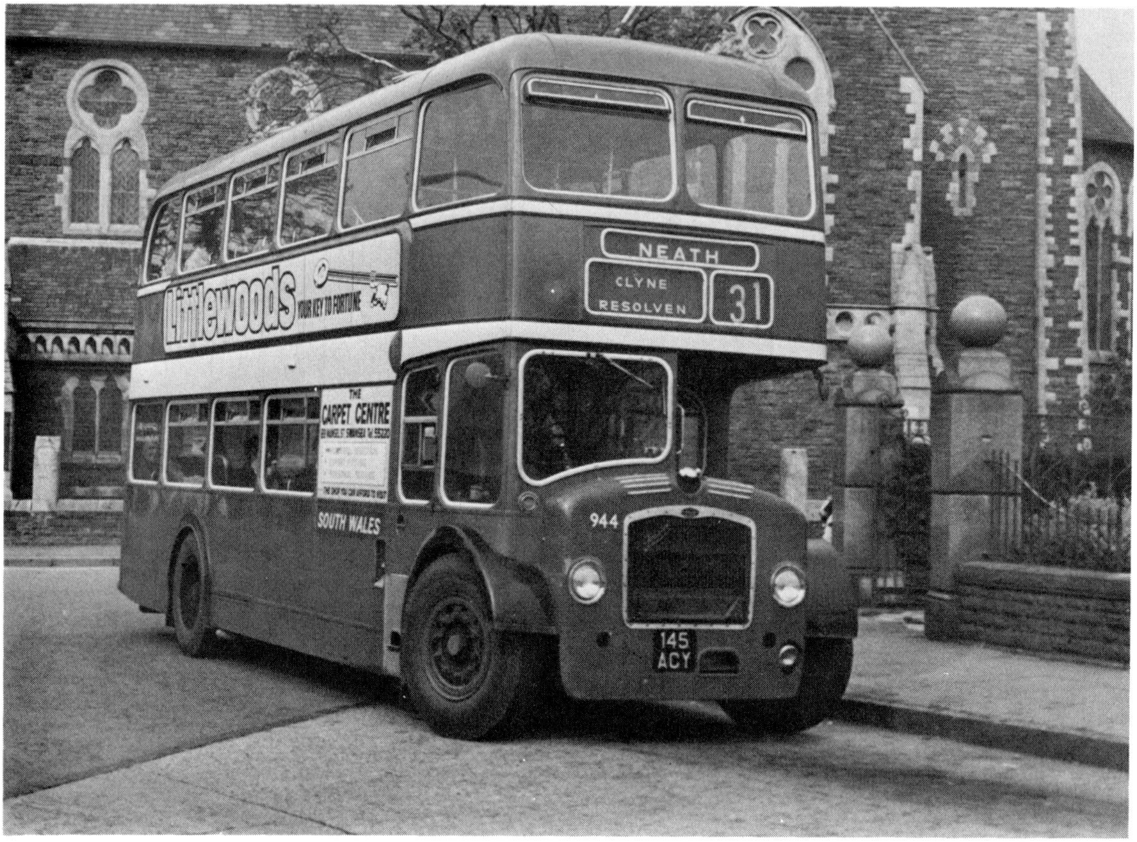
NEATH
CLYNE
RESOLVEN
31
Littlewoods
YOUR KEY TO FORTUNE
THE
CARPET CENTRE
SOUTH WALES
944
145
ACY

Chester's Eastgate Street—a favourite spot for jigsaw and cut-price painting manufacturers. Usually missing from these mass-produced views however is a Corporation Massey-bodied Foden PVD6, like the 1950 example seen here

Opposite, top: A Llandudno UDC 1951 Guy Wolf/Metalcraft passes units of the Great Orme railway, also owned by the council, in August, 1966

Opposite, bottom: A fine church in Neath diverts interest from this 1961 Bristol FSF6G built for United Welsh but displaying South Wales fleetnames in May, 1971 after the NBC reorganisation

24 HOUR
CLEANER
SERVICE
FIVE BELLS
8 BILLING ROAD
KINGSLEY ROAD
MOULTON
ELECTRICAL
DISTRIBUTORS LTD.
34
KINGSLEY PK.
TERRACE
Northampton
TEL-36158
ENH254D
KINGS HEATH
17
GNH259F

4 Buses at Rest

In some small towns it is still feasible for all bus services to terminate in one street and not cause undue dislocation to other traffic. Elsewhere, however, this has never been practicable and services terminate in different parts of the town centre. This makes life difficult for anyone making connections, so the answer may be found in the provision of a bus station. Many towns (and operators) were quick off the mark with these facilities but others still show a reticence. Not without reason however for a bus station must be placed where it is of maximum convenience to the public, i.e. where land is at a premium. On some services it must also create extra mileage across or around a busy town centre adding minutes to journey time and perhaps involving extra vehicle and crew costs. On the other hand the bus operator is offering improved facilities which may stem the loss of his passengers and he may well recoup the additional costs through all the adjuncts that can go with a bus station. Even the humble stop is now worth more than a flag. With increasingly wider headways shelters are becoming a necessity and advertising companies are willing to provide these free in exchange for the advertising rights. The planners have been here too and buses are often forced into laybys to pick up their intending passengers. All very well until the bus tries to move out again. . . . Author's pet hate? That non-feature of certain South Wales towns, unmarked stopping places—knowledge of which is apparently handed down from father to son to the complete bewilderment of visitors.

It is not always appreciated that the street tramcar outlived the petrol double-decker. Morecambe & Heysham was amongst the last operators of the type in Britain; a 1938 petrol AEC Regent/Park Royal loads in Heysham Road during June, 1954

Opposite: The magic of the bus at night. The crew have gone for a cuppa leaving their illuminated steed behind—perhaps saving you a long wait in the cold. Two Roe-bodied Daimler CVG6s of Northampton Corporation

Despite the arrival of several Leyland Titan PD2s in 1947, Accrington Corporation reverted to PD1s for its 1949 deliveries. 118 with East Lancs body, pauses near the bus station before continuing to the delightfully Lancashire destination of Oswaldtwistle in July, 1966. The Blackburn vehicle would be loading for its home town where Queen Victoria (below) still stares impassively towards the railway station. The smart lining-out of Blackburn Corporation Leyland-bodied TD4 39 in August, 1952 evidently fails to attract her attention

This Burton Guy Arab III of 1950 still carried its original Davies lowbridge bodywork when seen at Wetmore Bridge in April, 1952. Most of the bodies in this batch of both highbridge and lowbridge buses were later extensively rehabilitated but 18 was one of three that received new Massey bodies in 1960

There was a time when every good bus driver carried a piece of string 'just in case'. Here that essential item is seen holding down the bonnet of a Bedwas & Machen UDC Bedford OWB in July, 1949. The Bedford was connecting at Machen with the Western Welsh service to Newport in the days before the jointly-operated through service

The buses of Bedwas & Machen UDC are often seen hunting in pairs and these two early postwar Albion Venturers were found in Caerphilly in July, 1949. Both bodies were by Welsh Metal Industries to differing styles and were later heavily rebuilt

A memory of Pool Meadow bus station, Coventry before it was rebuilt. Waiting is one of the nine MAUDSLAY Regent IIIs with Metro-Cammell bodies supplied to the Corporation in 1951

A single-deck AEC Regent of Corvedale Motors near the Town Hall in Ludlow. The chassis is a rebuild by its previous owner, Don Everall—Burlingham built the bodywork

A new Northern Counties-bodied AEC Regent oiler leads two other Cardiff Corporation buses one crisp day in 1934

South Wales summed up in one picture. Cardiff AEC Bridgemaster 365 unloads at the Circle in Tredegar in July, 1962. One can almost hear the beat of the AV590 engine and smell the clutch fumes as the driver prepares for a hill start

Crosville vehicles wait to take up their duties in Wrexham bus station. Some of the variety still to be afforded by the Crosville fleet in September, 1959 can be seen in this view; the nearest vehicle is a 1934 Leyland Lion LT5A with postwar Burlingham bodywork

Derby Castle, Douglas where horse trams, motor buses and cars of the Manx Electric Railway still meet. All three are visible in the *Left* view showing one of two 1935 Vulcan toastracks once owned by Douglas Corporation. No1 is seen in postwar years with Bedford engine and radiator. Douglas also purchased two RT-type AEC Regents with Northern Counties bodies in 1947—at the time of writing similar provincial-type Regent IIIs still bear the brunt of the traffic.

Some of Crosville's earliest Lodekkas were fitted out as semi-luxury vehicles. DLB682 in Liverpool had received standard bus destination equipment and a later style of grille by the time this picture was taken however

Vertical-engined buses of traditional layout have never proved popular for one-man operation. However Darwen Leyland Tiger TS8 20 was doing just that in June, 1957, its Burlingham body having been suitably adapted

Purple Motors of Bethesda was using this all-Crossley double-decker owned by the associated Deiniolen fleet on its Bangor–Bethesda service in July, 1966. Seen here loading at Bangor, JC 9795 subsequently became the last all-Crossley in passenger service in Great Britain

The Derby trolleybus system had a number of attractive corners such as this spot in Ashbourne Road. A 1946 Sunbeam W/Park Royal to utility style on a short working in September, 1962

A Farsley Omnibus Roe-bodied Leyland PD3A/2 takes on passengers at Pudsey Bus Station on its service to Horsforth in March, 1968, the last month of operation before takeover by Leeds City Transport

The Park Royal bodies on the preselective Regent IIIs built for Halifax Corporation in the 1947–50 period were of composite construction and clearly based on the wartime design despite the well-rounded front profile. Hills and rather attractive stone shelters provide the background to 347 leaving the bus station in June, 1964

One of Leicester's six-wheel AEC Renowns in August, 1953, contrasts with the Renown on page 106. This was one of the 1940 batch with Metro-Cammell bodies intended to resemble the Northern Counties units on the previous series. The result was barely recognisable as Metro-Cammell; such rounded proportions have never been a feature of its own designs

The Harrington Cavalier is still considered widely as one of the finest coach designs ever. This 1960 example on AEC Reliance chassis was used on the express services of Neath & Cardiff Luxury Coaches Ltd. N&C was another former BET subsidiary that disappeared when the NBC revised its South Wales bus operations in January, 1971. The company actually ran beyond Neath to Swansea for most of its existence as this coach at Cardiff bus station reveals in June, 1966

Newark in June, 1940 with two Brush-bodied Leylands of the mid-thirties belonging to the Lincolnshire Road Car Co. Ltd. Reflecting the BET influence at that time, note the Federation style bodywork on the Tiger TS7, the Cub also shares the BET-style destination box

One of Nottingham's fine 8ft wide Brush-bodied BUT trolleybuses in May, 1963

A semi-utility Daimler CWA6/Park Royal of Leeds City Transport in the Central bus station. Several of these vehicles in later life received 1934 piano-front Roe bodies which, having been reconditioned, had outlasted their original AEC chassis

Midland Red has one of the largest territories in England. Above, wartime intruder 2439, an unfrozen Leyland Titan TD7/Northern Counties, stands outside Stafford railway station before its rebuilding. Fast electric trains are now available to Birmingham and prospective bus passengers have to change at Wolverhampton—even in the days of the TD7 and the through service it was necessary to rebook at that point. Over fifty miles to the south in the middle of nowhere at Malvern Wells is the attractive terminus of the frequent 144 service to Birmingham. Below the last of the 1965-registered D9s rests before the long run back in July, 1971

The valleys of South Wales mean plenty of hill climbing. A Gelligaer Leyland Tiger TS8 with Burlingham utility body is seen in Bargoed nearing the end of a hard life in May, 1956

Huddersfield Corporation's fine six-wheel trolleybuses were not only to be found amongst the town's solid buildings but also the open moorland surrounding it. One of the last prewar type Karriers to survive was this 1940 E6 which put in a further ten years after rebodying by Roe in 1953. 523 is parked outside the railway station in St George's Square in July, 1955, the lion checks trolley heads as they go by

Genteel Colwyn Bay in June, 1951. The AEC Regal III with Strachans bodywork to Tilling specification was an unusual addition to the Crosville fleet in 1948

For years the bodywork orders for City of Oxford Motor Services were split between Park Royal and Weymann, inevitably on AEC chassis. Two Regent IIs are seen in Banbury in the more profitable days of May, 1956. 843 is the Park Royal version, in this case resembling the semi-utility bodies also produced in 1946 for London Transport on the 100 Sutton Daimlers and for Southdown on Leyland chassis

Manchester's Piccadilly bus station before its reconstruction. The North Western Willowbrook rebodies of the early 50s on prewar Bristol K5G chassis are so well known that the similar examples on wartime Guy Arabs tend to be forgotten. No24 prepares for the twenty mile run to Northwich in Cheshire

'Twenty minutes only, please!' A Yelloway Leyland Tiger with Trans-United coachwork pauses at Derby bus station on its way back to Rochdale one rainy day in October, 1951

Classic Weymann styling, albeit slightly modernised, on this Newport Leyland TS8 is a far cry from today's Metro-Scanias which still use the bus station in Dock Street. The market forms a background virtually unchanged since this photograph was taken in September, 1952

Twenty years later Newport has nearly eliminated double-crew operation—Metro-Scania 25 loads in Dock Street in 1972

The trolley booms are hardly visible in this atmospheric 1933 view of new Notts & Derby trolleybus 321 thus heightening the motorbus appearance of these particular vehicles. The Metro-Cammell bodied AEC 661T stands at the Nottingham terminus on the corner of King St/Queen St ready for the run through cityscape and countryside to Ripley

A busy scene in Queen Street, Nottingham on the last day of the Notts & Derby trolleybus system, April 25, 1953. This 1949 BUT 9611T/Weymann, like the rest of the fleet at the closure, found its way to Bradford where, of course, it remained light blue and cream

Red & White buses are not such a familiar sight in Hereford bus station as they were in the early fifties. A centre-entrance Albion Valkyrie/Duple of 1938 leads a Gloucester-bound Guy Arab III/Duple in original livery

This 1936 Roe-bodied Leyland TTB4 although outwardly indistinguishable from the rest of the South Lancs trolleybus fleet was in fact one of only four owned by Bolton Corporation and operated by South Lancs on its behalf. Note the lamps hung haphazardly around the front panel. Bolton Town Hall provides the backdrop at Moor Lane in April, 1952

A concentration on mechanical maintenance during the war years caused Ribble to embark on a large scale rebodying programme in the late forties. Two Leylands with postwar Burlingham bodies in June, 1954, show the varying nature of the company's territory. Above a 1935 Tiger TS7 stands at Coniston, just inside Lancashire, before returning through lakeland to Ambleside, whilst below a 1938 Titan TD5 loads in Preston

A 1950 Barnaby-bodied Leyland Comet of Reliance (R. Store Ltd) awaits its next load at Christ Church, Doncaster

Mid-Wales Motorways used to be a much larger enterprise than it is today. In August, 1962, a Guy Arab with Burlingham body reminiscent of early Ribble White Ladies is a reminder of the days when Mid-Wales double-deckers ran into Barker Street, Shrewsbury

Stratford-upon-Avon in June, 1961 before the tourists moved in and the prices went up. Lazy days of afternoon jaunts on the river, rich ices, and immaculate blue and cream all-Leyland PD2 double-deckers with silver roofs glistening in the sunshine. Local councillors strongly protested in 1969 when it was learned that Stratford Blue was to be absorbed by Midland Red, claiming that the blue buses were as famous as the red ones of London

A duplicate for Stevensons of Uttoxeter's ex-London Craven RT in the form of this Park Royal-bodied Guy at Burton bus station in March, 1961. It is pleasing to record that double-deckers are still required on this semi-rural service

More memories. A new Stratford Blue PD2/ Willowbrook on the Stratford–Birmingham service operated jointly with Midland Red stands amongst the latter's LD8s clustered under St. Martins-in-the-Bull Ring, Birmingham in May, 1956. Since then the Bull Ring has been rebuilt beyond recognition and now incorporates a Midland Red bus station; thus virtually ending the days of services terminating in different parts of the city centre

Smiths Safety Services was an early operator in Lincolnshire which ran between Skegness and Boston. Its Leyland-bodied Lion waits on Scarborough Avenue, Skegness in July, 1930

In complete contrast are Standerwick's sleek ECW-bodied Bristol VRs used on long-distance services. The prototype and a production vehicle declare an intention to run to Birmingham whilst parked amidst the mêlée at the Coliseum bus station, Blackpool in September, 1972

Most bus stations have an area where vehicles not required immediately can be parked out of the way. The photographer was lucky to catch all three Douglas Corporation CWA6s opposite the bus station in July, 1969; the Duple bodies were in remarkably original condition after nearly a quarter-of-a-century's service

I've heard of 'dial-a-ride', but this is ridiculous! A withdrawn Todmorden Leyland-bodied PD2 still proves as useful around the bus station in April, 1963 as its two more serviceable companions. The FWT-registered vehicles were amongst the first PD2s to be built (1947)

A 1938 Daimler COG5 and a 1937 AEC Regent of Trent parked behind Derby bus station in the mid-fifties. Both carry postwar bodies by Willowbrook replacing the original front-entrance Weymann units

A long-lived Leyland-bodied PD2/12 of the newly-formed Calderdale undertaking reverses out at Burnley bus station shortly before the heavens opened one bleak day in May, 1972. The 1951 Titan, still in Todmorden livery but with new numbers, misses with ease a fellow PD2 of Burnley, Colne & Nelson twelve years its junior and with equally well-proportioned Northern Counties bodywork

A Widnes Leyland Lion LT7/Massey of 1935 parks outside the Parish Church in St Paul's Road near the Town Hall termini in August, 1950

A 1935 Eastern Counties-bodied Bristol GO5G with West Yorkshire's characteristic 'tin-bible' indicator awaits passengers for Keighley at Bradford in September, 1936

The 'bible' indicators had been replaced with blinds of standard postwar Tilling style by the time these two JO5Gs were photographed at Bradford bus station in July, 1948. No965, right, was later the subject of a most interesting reconstruction by West Yorkshire—the chassis was extended at the front and the engine mounted forward of the axle, the resulting vehicle seating 43 people

One of North Western's fleet of 1929–31 Tilling-Stevens that were rebodied in the mid-thirties by Eastern Counties to this half-canopy style, typical North Western of the period. 536 awaits its next duty in Stockport during August, 1949

Two vehicles of William Truman & Sons at its Mansfield terminus in May, 1952. A Daimler CVD6/Northern Coachbuilders leads a Crossley/Burlingham —Trumans was acquired by East Midland in 1956

Plans to convert Barnsley bus station to end-on-loading had not been announced when this Yorkshire Traction Leyland was seen there in July, 1971. Rebuilt from a PS2 single-deck chassis in 1961, the new Roe body incorporated parts of Bridgemaster origin to rather unhappy proportions partly disguised by the non-standard livery

The West Bridgford bus undertaking was absorbed by nearby Nottingham Corporation in September, 1968. Still in stock at the time of takeover was this 1948 AEC Regent III—very much the provincial RT with its preselective gearbox and four-bay Park Royal body incorporating half-drop windows in the usual RT positions. No5 is seen at Trent Boulevard/Seymour Road, in June, 1953

A delicious pair of Yorkshire Woollen District Roe-bodied Leylands in the days when the maroon was relieved by three cream bands. *Above:* A TD5 stands in Chester St. bus station, Bradford in July, 1948 with prewar West Yorkshire Bristols to its right and a Ledgard Daimler at the rear. *Left:* Dewsbury bus station looks splendidly 'period' as it supplies a new PD2 with passengers in May, 1950. An atmospic, to use the latest descriptive jargon

Two specially-equipped Fodens for hill work. *Right:* A West Mon Foden/ Willowbrook storms down Bargoed Hill amidst a cloud of exhaust fumes in July, 1962. *Below:* A Llandudno Foden/Metalcraft climbs the Great Orme near St Tudno's Church one fine day in August, 1966, any rolling back and it would be a dip in the drink for both bus and passengers! Sprag equipment was fitted to prevent this

5 Made to Measure

EVERY BUS OPERATOR can tell you of at least one tight spot on his services. Rarely however does it reach the stage that a specially designed or fitted fleet of vehicles has to be acquired which is just as well as the effect on the price must be disheartening. A number of examples does exist though, probably the best-known being East Yorkshire's double-deckers which until recently required specially-shaped roof domes to fit under the gothic arch of the Beverley Bar. Fortunately for East Yorkshire, but unfortunately for transport photographers, there is now a way round the Bar so these unusual vehicles are dying out.

Not all obstacles are man-made, nature has presented some operators with headaches too. Steep hills frequently call for high-powered or even specially-equipped vehicles to measure up to them. No other British bus route could compete with the hazards of West Mon's Bargoed Hill service however, which climbed 1220ft at 1 in 8, 500ft at 1 in 5, and 250ft at 1 in 4¼. Extra attractions on the hill included a low narrow railway bridge immediately followed by two sharp turns, the first to the right and then to the left. Specially-equipped buses had to be used of course, but thankfully a deviation ended operations up the hill in November, 1963.

Low bridges afflict many services, so much so that lowheight buses are nothing special. Much rarer however are lowbridge trolleybuses but St Helens had several including this Ransomes showing off when new

South Wales purchased eight single-deck Regent Vs with special Roe bodies for work in the Llanelli dock area. No38 dating from 1963 demonstrates why orthodox underfloor-engined vehicles were unsuitable—the Regent Vs replaced Regals that were themselves specially low built

Apparently much to the awe of local cyclists, an East Yorkshire Leyland TD3/ Brush with Gothic roofline squeezes through the Beverley Bar in June, 1938. The three windows at the front of the upper deck are a further distinctive touch

When the last of North Western's traditional front-engined single-deckers fell due for withdrawal in 1964, new vehicles with specially shaped roofs had to be acquired to operate under the Bridgewater Canal at Dunham Woodhouses. The initial vehicles, Bedford VALs with Strachans bodies (above), were themselves replaced in 1971 by Bristol RELL6Ls whose ECW bodies (below) were an intriguing variation on the standard. With the splitting up of North Western's bus operations in 1972, the RELLs passed with the service to Crosville. It may be imagination but vegetation seems to have increased between September, 1964 when the Bedford was photographed and August, 1972, the date of the Bristol picture

WIGAN
WIGAN CORPORATION
JP-3707
AEK-511

GOODWIN'S Extra FLOUR
MIDLAND
3820
SAXA

6 Around the Garages

Anyone interested in buses is bound to be attracted to garages. It is difficult to resist the temptation to step inside but the visitor should always immediately ascertain whether his presence is convenient and not be surprised if it is not. Bodies such as the Omnibus Society and the P.S.V. Circle run properly organised trips to operators when there is always someone on hand to give his verdict on various types in the fleet.

Undertakings with only one garage are usually the most interesting as every job right up to major body and chassis overhaul has to be carried out under the one roof. Practices vary from one concern to another but generally vehicles are swept out every night and washed every other day. An eye is kept on the electrical items to see they are all functioning properly and all vehicles go over the pits at regular intervals for inspection. Drivers, of course, should report any defects that develop during the working day. High mileages in all conditions plus mechanical washing mean buses need repainting rather more often than private cars, and this is usually carried out every two to three years.

A new vehicle is granted a Certificate of Fitness which lasts for seven years after which it must be thoroughly overhauled for re-certification. The body will then be made as good as new and the opportunity taken to strip down the mechanical units completely. Not surprisingly successive certificates are usually granted for ever-decreasing periods. In the provinces bodies are not normally removed for overhaul although it may be necessary after serious accident damage. However the author has come across this practice in his recent travels. Needless to say the vehicles concerned were getting on in years, fifteen in fact, but the chassis were of a solid, reliable make and the bodies whilst needing some attention were not of the light-weight type so the machines were well worth overhauling. One advantage was that engine and body fitters were able to proceed without getting in each other's way. The reconditioned chassis has to be seen to be believed and the completed vehicles were naturally to a very high standard, still a good advertisement to the fleet concerned.

Bus washing in the fifties. The army of men (note the 'gaffer') involved in the washing of the Wigan buses, above, had been replaced at the Midland Red garage, left, by one man and a machine. Incidentally the sleek design of the Midland Red D5B was based on a wartime prototype

This Caerphilly wartime Guy with Roe bodywork had gone up in the world in July, 1962. Hydraulic lifts such as this particularly aid chassis cleaning and spraying

Mechanics get to grips with this magnificent Leyland Tiger of Fishwicks in 1946

Maintenance Blackburn style in May, 1972. Corporation Guy Arabs undergo routine maintenance over the pits whilst the East Lancs body of 157, below, is thoroughly overhauled prior to re-marrying with its dependable Guy Arab chassis, surely one of Britain's most underrated motorbus designs. On re-entry into service 157 was painted in a revised livery based on that of Blackburn's Atlanteans, a modified version of which was subsequently adopted as standard for rear-entrance buses

All maintenance completed, vehicles are then lined up for the next day's service. Here a City of Oxford Motor Services lowbridge Regent V stands alongside an Aldershot & District Dennis Loline borrowed to cover a temporary vehicle shortage in May, 1969. Both bodies were by East Lancs

James garage at Ammanford was used as a bus station during the day so off-service vehicles had to be parked in a nearby side street. A Strachans-bodied Leyland Tiger PS1 heads the line-up in June, 1956

Some operators favour open parking, balancing the increased deterioration of vehicles with the high cost of buildings. Open parking would be doing little harm to this Crossley/Willowbrook at the Haverfordwest garage of Western Welsh one sunny day in August, 1961. Cold mornings are a different proposition though as this 1949 Salmesbury-bodied Foden clearly demonstrates as it coughs into life at Whieldon's Green Bus garage, Rugeley in March, 1964

Barton vehicles, self-made and converted! Falling in the latter category is this 1939 petrol Leyland Lion/Duple converted to run on gas during the war. Below, Barton built the bodywork itself on this Viewmaster—the chassis was officially designated a Barton BTS1 but was in fact constructed from a pair of old Leyland chassis, in this case ex-Burnley, Colne & Nelson. 634 in the now-closed Huntingdon Street bus station, Nottingham in February, 1952

7 Dedicated to the Self-Made and the Converted

If ever a fleet was self-made, it is the company which dominates so much of this book's area—Midland Red, or the Birmingham & Midland Motor Omnibus Co. to give the full title. The company grew in the twenties and thirties under the combined genius of traffic manager O. C. Power and chief engineer L. G. Wyndham Shire. Buses of the company's own manufacture were first constructed in 1923 under the name SOS, the initials standing for "Shire's Own Specification". With the benefit of being both operator and designer, SOS models were consistently ahead of their time and ideally suited to the job, a large number were also built in prewar years for financially-associated companies. After the war, the initials became BMMO, an abbreviation of the company's full title, and advanced designs continued to appear until production ceased in 1970, the long line killed partly by loss of labour tempted away by the high wages offered in local car factories.

Manufacture of chassis and engines by operators is not surprisingly rare but more common is the introduction of non-standard engines into well-known chassis. Apart from Midland Red a number of other operators has also built its own bodywork at various times.

Barton Transport has demonstrated a remarkable talent for constructions and conversions over the years, but probably reached its peak in the early fifties with its Viewmasters. These comprised old Leyland chassis rebuilt to 30ft length, often by joining the front half of one to the rear of another, and then fitting new bodywork usually of the operator's own manufacture.

The field of conversions and reconstructions is particularly rich. A bus may be rebuilt to another pattern to avoid buying a new vehicle of an untried style, the reconstruction perhaps being prompted by accident damage. The early postwar years also produced quite a crop of unusual reconstructions to reduce the desperate vehicle shortage. Lengthening to take advantage of the revised box dimensions was favoured by a number of operators including (besides Barton and Midland Red), Preston Corporation and Trent, whose Titans and Regals respectively were extensively modified in other ways during rebuilding. Finally worth mentioning under conversions are the open-top buses of various seaside resorts (often vehicles which would otherwise have been pensioned off and thus of extra special interest) and the unusual combinations derived by the sinister-sounding practice of body swapping.

One of Midland Red's own 1938 FEDD models was fitted with this modified front end in 1942 as a prototype for the postwar fleet. The traditional radiator and wings were reinstated when the Brush bodywork was thoroughly rebuilt, along with the rest of the batch, in the early fifties. Walsall bus station still looks much the same although the 118 stand has been repositioned, the trolleybus wires have come and gone, and FEDD 2167 has unfortunately gone too

Trent was a keen user of SOS models before the war. This ON model was one of 12 with Duple bodies specially purchased in 1934 to compete against Barton's Lions on the Derby–Nottingham road. 503 was rebuilt with AEC 7·7 oil engine and new Willowbrook body in the forties as seen here near Mount St bus station, Nottingham

Two Warrington Corporation Fodens were given PRE-WAR Metro-Cammell/Crossley bodies, attractive in themselves but an aesthetic disaster with that bonnet design—note the need for a projecting cab! However the idea was sound, those pre-lightweight Metro-Cammell bodies were remarkably durable whilst the new Foden chassis must have been a better proposition than the original worn-out Crossley Mancunians. Five Leyland PD1s received similar bodies. No36 in April, 1953

Another interesting body-swap. Daimler 168 was the first of several Doncaster Daimlers and Leylands to receive Roe bodies from withdrawn trolleybuses. Enterprising Silcox of Pembroke Dock carried out two similar conversions many years earlier by fitting ex-Birmingham trolleybus bodies to new Bristol K6G chassis even retaining the full-fronts

Several Preston Corporation Leyland-bodied PD2s of the early fifties have been lengthened to 30ft and at the same time converted to front-entrance. Early examples were from lowbridge models and look rather odd in their new highbridge guise but No61 here was built as a highbridge vehicle, the pleasantly proportioned style giving us some idea of what Leyland bodies might have looked like had they remained in production longer. Like all the reconstructions, 61 was re-registered and now carries a 1965 mark. It leaves the new Preston bus station with its curious rounded walls one baking day in July, 1972

This 1946 Guy Arab II/ Northern Counties of Potteries Motor Traction was rebuilt to front-entrance layout after a serious accident. Thus reconstructed PMT gained useful operating experience of this configuration before taking delivery of new front-entrance vehicles

Looking more like an escapee from fellow seaside town Bournemouth, the Burlingham body of Blackpool Corporation PD2 305 reveals an experimental two-door layout complete with twin staircases for pay-as-you-enter (two-man) operation in October, 1960

Two double-deckers with experimental Ruston & Hornsby air-cooled engines which account for the eccentric radiator designs. NorthWestern Weymann-bodied 555 is barely recognisable as a PD2 near Mersey Square, Stockport in August, 1965 whilst below Lincoln 23 stands rather self-consciously at the entrance to the depot in September, 1962. The latter is a 1948 Guy Arab III with body built by Guy itself to Park Royal design

Surrounded by a wide range of types in May 1949 is a Sheffield A fleet AEC Regent with body constructed in 1940 by the transport department's own workshops. The grim background of sooty buildings has gone fortunately to be replaced by a vista of tower flats. The vehicles have disappeared too although the variety still remains

The construction of Clifton housing estate gave West Bridgford UDC a slight headache as lowbridge vehicles had to be acquired quickly. To partly overcome the problem two prewar Regents had their Park Royal bodies rebuilt to lowbridge layout by **Willowbrook. No9, suitably converted, loads in Broad Marsh bus station, Nottingham in June, 1953**

Lincolnshire ran four ancient Vulcan toastracks along Skegness sea front for years. Their replacements were just as unorthodox and equally distinctive, comprising Bedford OBs whose standard Duple Vista bodies were rebuilt as shown for their new task. 2094 started life with Western National during 1950 and looks very refreshing in its later form at Ingoldmells beach in August, 1964

Left: Thanks to faultless maintenance Lytham St. Annes always gets full value from its vehicles which often last years after similar types have disappeared elsewhere. Regrettably short-lived as an open-topper though was this particularly attractive conversion of Leyland Titan TD4 46 seen in 1960, still with gearless transmission after 23 years. The full-width cab is an original feature of the Leyland bodywork—a rare example of that factory departing from its standard design

Right: **Morecambe & Heysham's open-toppers must be the most garish in the country. The destination blind of 58, a 1949 Regent III/Park Royal, looks quite insignificant—note the even less obvious service number in the front upper deck window**

Conductors pose with their Regents. The guard of Bullock & Sons 149 is completely overshadowed by his charge, itself about to be obscured by other vehicles including a Weymann-bodied AEC Q also of B. & S. *Right:* Bradford 421 stands in Forster Square in March, 1950 with the Transport offices to the left and the Post Office to the right. The curious window louvres on the Weymann bodywork were a typical Bradford feature

8 Smile Please!

YEARS AGO THE ACT OF PHOTOGRAPHING A BUS caused quite a stir both amongst platform staff and passers-by. No wonder the crews look vaguely suspicious in many of these pictures. Life is easier for the photographer nowadays, the relative cheapness of the pastime has made it more widespread and the busman now accepts having his picture taken as part of the job. Quite often he will strike up a conversation, always of great interest to the layman. The older hands are usually the most talkative and will have many memories to make the chat worthwhile. He will tell you that he was "passed out" on some ancient AEC and confirm that those chaps up at head office really are mad—they should never have thrown out those three-axle Crossleys with bucket seats you were so keen on. Comments regarding head office are always fairly virulent and very often should be taken with a pinch of salt. In small undertakings everyone knows the "gaffer" but larger ones can tend towards remoteness of command with adverse results. Nobody likes taking orders from a faceless signature so it does help if "authority" can occasionally manifest itself as ordinary flesh and blood. Many large undertakings produce excellent staff magazines and it saddened many to see those of NBC companies disappear to be replaced by a national magazine however good—the sheet of local news is no substitute for some of those house journals.

Bus strikes are comparatively rare despite the working conditions and the inferior pay. Yet because of the widespread inconvenience they cause, strikes by public service employees always upset people more than those by factory workers even though the latter may be causing more harm. Not many would care to conduct on an "open-back" in winter—but how many busmen would swap their relative independence on the road to join the production line rat race? Buses get into your blood—possibly earlier than you think. A Rhymney woman recently wrote to a daily newspaper stating that whilst she was "expecting" she had this uncontrollable desire to inhale motor fuels. She used to pop down to the local bus terminus every day and there satisfy her cravings—strange to relate the baby she was carrying eventually became a bus driver!

The conductor changes the destination of Hull unfrozen Regent 199, one of many wartime Hull buses to receive prewar bodies in later life, in this case a Weymann unit off a 1937 Daimler COG5. Guy 220, alongside, retained its austerity Park Royal to the end however as seen in May, 1959

A Leicester City Transport conductor glowers at the photographer in September, 1966, perhaps gloomily contemplating that he is one of a disappearing race. The vehicle is an East Lancs-bodied AEC Renown

The drivers of these two Bedford QLs on Southport's beach service have only each other for company one depressing day in the early fifties. The QLs were rebuilt from army lorries and were unique to Southport Corporation

Time for a quick smoke at Meir Square before returning through the Five Towns on PMT's so-called 'main line' service. The wartime Daimler CWA6 chassis put in good service for the Potteries, being one of several acquired with the business of Browns, of Tunstall, and fitted with new lightweight Northern Counties bodies in 1954. Business looked particularly good in 1961

The driver of this Samuel Ledgard Leyland argues a point with an unseen victim in Leeds in September, 1962. The Leyland-bodied PD2 had always been in independent ownership having recently arrived from the immaculate Felix, of Hatfield, fleet

Short back and sides for the conductor of Woolliscroft's Silver Service Willowbrook-bodied Daimler COG5/40. New in 1938 and seen in Matlock 17 years later the bus had still many years of life left and eventually clocked well over a million miles

Conductor changes destinations at the highest village in England, a North Western L5G/Weymann turns at Flash in October, 1963. The post office is named after the parish

'You're all right there, Dai.' A Caerphilly Leyland Leopard with Massey body of somewhat severe appearance squeezes between two Vauxhalls in June, 1969, the driver taking extra care not to damage the special livery commemorating the investiture of Prince Charles

Conductor delves into his cashbag of period pieces like half-crowns, tanners and threepenny bits before boarding that least utilitarian of wartime combinations—Daimler CWA6 chassis and Northern Counties body. Widnes 54 stands in Mersey Road under the gantry to the old transporter bridge, now replaced, before making a journey due north across the town in August, 1957

WINTON
AMV 124
GROSVENOR
SNACK BAR.
OWEN BROS
RETAIL
TOBACCONIS

WORTH'S
ENSTONE
JO 2351

9 Buses and People

THERE'S NOWT AS QUEER AS FOLK, and folk are transport's lifeblood. Those who have the misfortune to deal with the general public for any length of time will know why new bus crews soon develop that look of vague hostility—some people are only too ready to take advantage of a youngster inexperienced in handling people. It can thus be gathered that relations between the public and the staff of large undertakings in particular are not as good as they might be. Irrespective of whoever started the spiral of deteriorating relations and assuming that many passengers will remain mean, inconsiderate, impatient, muddle-headed and even violent, what can bus operators do to improve matters?

Before joining the transport industry the author mistakenly spent his first few working months in the retail trade which, if nothing else, taught him the importance of looking after the customer properly. It is too much to expect a busman issuing 80 fares in a few minutes to lavish that "you-are-the-only-person-in-the-world-that-matters" smile on everybody but those responsible for their training should at least impress on new recruits that passengers are really customers who may well spend around £50 a year in the "shop". Stunts like leaving timing points several minutes early or ignoring potential passengers running towards the stop are unnecessary and not likely to encourage further bus travel. The courteous drivers of West Yorkshire's experimental "Chauffeur Coach" service in Harrogate are a giant step in the right direction.

Larger operators find it worthwhile to have a public relations department, often headed by someone specially trained in this difficult sphere. The department will handle inquiries and complaints, and away from the pressures of working on the road should always provide the standard of service and politeness expected in a shop. It is worth noting that passengers rarely complain about the age of the vehicles they travel in, nearly all complaints refer to the service provided.

Opposite, top: Everybody on. . . . Cue for a queue for a Q! Sharp's AEC Q loads up near Exchange Station, Manchester in 1936

Opposite, below: Everybody off. . . . An ex-City of Oxford 1931 Regal with later Duple coachwork belonging to Worths of Enstone does the opposite manoeuvre sometime during the war

West Mon might like to think that the crowds and the flags were out in September, 1952 for its East Lancs rebodied wartime Guy. Unfortunately the main attraction was apparently Wilfred Pickles who was visiting High Street, Blackwood that day!

Back to the days when children were seen but not heard. A small girl watches a Chesterfield Corporation gearless Tiger with Metro-Cammell bodywork leave the bus station in June, 1936. A perfect example of the prewar municipal single-decker, like children it too was less likely to be heard than today's versions

What choice vehicles have stood in the square beneath the walls of Caernarvon Castle. The standard early postwar Eastern Coach Works body was of more modern appearance than most of its contemporaries so it comes as an ever greater surprise to find it on this positively vintage Leyland Titan TD1 chassis, albeit modernised with Covrad radiator. A toothless potential customer and his good lady contemplate Clynnog & Trevor's ex-Southern Vectis machine in June, 1956

Be at peace with your pipe. A holidaymaker in full steam ponders over the Colwyn Bay 1937 Guy Wolf with the Wolverhampton registration. Having come some considerable way to sample the fresh air it seems vaguely ludicrous to pollute oneself with pipesmoke!

A small boy peers out at the buses near his home in August, 1949. A dusky Leyland-bodied TD5 of Accrington Corporation indicates that repainting programmes had still not caught up after the difficulties of the war years

Utter chaos seems to surround these two Leyland-bodied PD2s of Widnes Corporation on a private hire trip. Despite the decade difference in construction dates, the family resemblance to the Accrington TD5 above is quite clear

A lady in a ghastly tartan coat squeezes through the rear door of this Rawtenstall Corporation Leyland TS8 in the centre of the town in April, 1954. The single-deck Leyland body of the late thirties with its small windows did not have quite the classic appeal of the contemporary double-decker. Note the fog and headlamp combination

A little lad finds the steps steep on this 'Loot' (Lancashire United Transport) Guy Arab III with Roe body at Leeds in August, 1949

The long queue in the background ignores the Scarborough Promenade bus in July, 1950. This is one of several Leyland TS8s fitted with the special 1936 Plaxton bodies originally mounted on 1928 ADC 425-type chassis

After retiring from the murk of Salford in 1962, this 1947 AEC Regent III/Metro-Cammell spent its last few years in the Grimsby–Cleethorpes fleet. No37 on Cleethorpes seafront in August, 1964

This former Wigan TD2 found its way into the Lincolnshire fleet in 1947 and two years later was still considered sufficiently sound to receive this new body by Roe. Unusually for postwar TD2 rebodies, the old radiator was retained. 1607 stands in Newark bus station in July, 1954; after withdrawal the body was transferred to a Regent II

10 Omnibus Shuffle

THE RATE AT WHICH BUSES CHANGE HANDS has rarely been brisker than at the present time. This is partly due to the NBC's rationalisation of companies and their operating areas which has brought many interesting vehicle transfers. In addition, the secondhand market is buoyant despite, or perhaps because of, the Government's bus grant scheme which has made new vehicles cheaper than for many years. The high cost of labour has had an effect too, when new vehicles are delayed many operators now find it more economic to buy a good secondhand vehicle with time left on its certificate of fitness rather than overhaul one of their own stock whose "ticket" has expired. The sale of relatively modern machines that have proved unsatisfactory in use has stimulated the market too. This is a very different situation to that prevailing only a few years ago. In the early sixties the acquisition of older vehicles by a large operator was a major event—and apart from the transfers of sound trolleybuses amongst the few remaining operators of those fine machines, the secondhand market was virtually the preserve of the under-capitalised independents. A takeover of another operator, usually a small independent, was normally the only other reason that older vehicles entered the fleet of a large undertaking and being non-standard they were generally soon sold off.

The early sixties were themselves a marked contrast to the late forties when the postwar travel boom was only handicapped by a desperate vehicle shortage. Operators lucky enough to obtain new buses soon found ready buyers large and small for any runners they were able to dispose of.

The coach market is rather different. The coaching business lays a greater emphasis on new vehicles so the turnover is naturally higher. Those coach operators who also run bus services often relegate their older coaches to stage carriage to finish their years, otherwise new owners have to be found. Seaside proprietors often run fleets of old coaches, the seasonal nature of their traffic means it is not worth buying new vehicles, and provided they are well-maintained the happy holidaymaker will forgive them not being of the latest type. The remainder will end their days alongside former service buses on works and school services or in the hands of building contractors.

Looking at first glance like a typical London street scene, these two well-maintained Craven RTs were actually working for Beckett, of Bucknall, in September, 1961. Beckett was acquired by PMT in 1963—the Essoldo in Hanley has gone too

Another escapee from London. This wartime Guy/Park Royal still with minute headlamps was enjoying a quieter life in Lancaster in June, 1954

An escapee from Lancaster this time! This Leyland PS1 with unmistakable Crossley body features was only twelve years old when Lytham St Annes acquired it in 1959

Barton purchased a large number of secondhand Leyland Titan PD1s between 1959 and 1961 to assist with fleet replacement. Typically they came from all over the country, this Massey-bodied example seen at The Rushes, Loughborough in September, 1962 originated with Birkenhead Corporation

Vehicles replaced included these fine Roe-bodied Leyland TD5s dating back to the late thirties, seen on Mount Street bus park, Nottingham in April, 1959. Although of similar specification, the vehicle on the left started life with Hebble and its companion with West Riding

Another former West Riding vehicle to have a long innings was this Roe-bodied Leyland Cub still with Pritchard, of Newborough, Anglesey, and seen near the garage as recently as July, 1966

A real gem in the Yorkshire Traction fleet in August, 1952 was this one-time Doncaster Leyland Titanic six-wheeler acquired with the services of Cawthornes. The body is a fine example of Roe 'architecture'. The attractive layout of red and cream still standard in 1972 unfortunately seems doomed under recent NBC directives

Another secondhand Leyland in the 'Tracky' fleet—not so impressive but a little faster! This 1960 Atlantean/Weymann came with the Mexborough & Swinton undertaking

This Crossley with 1953 Roe body of Wood, Mirfield was new to Baxter, Airdrie in 1949. Photographed at Dewsbury with a rather faded blind in July, 1963, it was to remain a welcome part of the local scene for a good few years after

Leicester exchanged some Regent IIs with Devon General for 1946 Weymann-bodied Regals like this. How about that 2d flat fare!

Other Leicester Regents found their way into the Hull Corporation fleet. This MkIII with Metro-Cammell body is seen in the Paragon bus station followed by an ex-St Helens RT

United Welsh bought a large number of secondhand Bristols in the early sixties to expedite standardisation on that make. This LL6B came from Thames Valley and is seen at Neath in September, 1964

Amongst vehicles ousted were these Leyland Royal Tigers with Bristol bodies which were snapped up by Red & White, being very similar to the large fleet it already had in stock. Note the sliding door ahead of the front axle

The former Bury Corporation Guy Wulfrunian/Roe has been fortunate in finding a succession of new owners. Seen in October, 1964 with Wrights, of Penycae, it leaves Wrexham bus station homeward bound

The early postwar secondhand purchases by Nottingham City Transport to ease its severe vehicle shortage are now very much a memory. A particularly choice example was this ex-West Bridgford 1930 Ransomes-bodied AEC Regent very similar to those supplied to London General (ST class) and East Surrey in particular. Almost as interesting is the ex-Halifax Regent/Park Royal behind. Both were seen on football specials parked off the Trent Embankment in June, 1948

Lancaster acquired these 1953 AEC Regal IVs from Rochdale Corporation in 1957, the Burlingham bodies originally having two doors. Nice to see 'please' used in the request to pay the driver in July, 1966

An all-Leyland TD2 of Eynon, Trimsaran in Llanelly during September, 1952. Ex-James of Ammanford, the body had been rebuilt by Jefferies

The Bradford trolleybus network received several useful shots in the arm through the purchase of secondhand vehicles and equipment from abandoned systems. This 1947 Weymann-bodied BUT seen at the 46 terminus in September, 1962 hailed from the Brighton Corporation fleet

The 'Afan Belle'. Thomas Bros. of Port Talbot was a comparatively recent convert to the open-top movement commencing in 1960. This 1940 Bristol K5G was one of two acquired that year—the decapitation of the ECW body and the fitting of the lower postwar type PV2 radiator was carried out by the previous owner, Brighton, Hove & District which ran several in this form for many years

It is most exceptional for an Irish vehicle to re-enter service on this side of the water. However in the early fifties Yeomans of Canon Pyon was running this Leyland Titan TD1 which started out with H.M.S. Catherwood, Belfast and was taken over by the Northern Ireland Road Transport Board (an ancestor of Ulsterbus) which evidently fitted a replacement body of its own design. AZ 7949 in Hereford bus station

This all-Leyland TD1 had an interesting life. Built for Ribble in 1930, it passed to Wilts & Dorset in 1939 to assist with the conveyance of workmen constructing and enlarging the military camps. Construction completed, the Titan moved again to Bristol and in 1948 yet again to Crosville. Despite its hectic career, it still had sufficient energy to serve the North Wales coast for several more seasons including Colwyn Bay in June, 1951

A vehicle crisis in the PMT fleet caused the wholesale purchase of secondhand buses during 1952. This ex-Halifax 8·8 litre AEC Regent/Roe seen at Derby bus station in June of that year was rushed into service without being repainted

GKV 97

28
HERDINGS
Sheffield
transport
699
DAIMLER
699
HWJ 699J

11 The Future

"Will the Minister consider the better and greater use of electric traction? The greatest mistake was to get rid of the trolley bus."

Mr David Stoddart M.P.

"I am not at all sure that the day will not come when we re-invent the tram and if that happens it will be a singularly bright feature in our march through technological revolution."

Mr John Peyton, Minister for Transport Industries

No, not a meeting of bus enthusiasts but Parliament in November 1972 discussing the very real possibility of a worldwide oil crisis developing within the next ten years. Had the trolleybus lasted a few more years it probably would have become a permanent feature of the urban scene, the new found ecology movement would never have allowed the replacement of those silent, fume-free machines. Current experiments with battery buses show there is still much development work to do, so can the traditional trolley stage a comeback?

Meanwhile a second generation of rear-engined vehicles is being evolved, such as the Leyland National and Metro-Scania, including some to "silent" specification. The ability of certain existing rear-engined models to ignite themselves has not exactly endeared them to operators, indeed the legend "passengers alight at centre exit" has taken on a more sinister meaning! The preoccupation with having the engine anywhere but the front has been made respectable with one-man operation, and the latter will continue to spread although the London decision to defer further one-manning may result in a provincial backlash.

Currently receiving much attention are city centre services like pedestrian precinct and park-and-ride buses, whether these will become a standard part of the transport scene or are merely a passing fancy only

Opposite, top: Last journey for most buses is to the scrapyard. This Daimler CVD6 was the pride of the Coventry fleet in 1950. The Metro-Cammell body, built with fluorescent lighting, bore a strong resemblance to Birmingham vehicles of the period. By 1966 it was still sound but considered too small, too cold and too old-fashioned so it had to go

Opposite, below: Typical of modern double-deckers is this Sheffield one-man equipped Daimler Fleetline with attractive deep window Park Royal bodywork incorporating two doors. Intended to speed loading and unloading, centre-exits in practice suffer from the delaying effects of poor visibility from the driver's cab further hampered by the safety timelag devices often fitted. Two-door buses are already losing favour with many operators—first stage passed on that one-way trip to the breakers?

time and rates money will tell—certainly the only ones to have been a roaring success are the free city centre buses of Nottingham. Ordinary urban services will continue to be the busman's bread-and-butter. The bus operator can make his contribution to smooth running with radio control whilst hoping for more priority schemes such as bus lanes and bus-actuated traffic lights (the mind boggles). The passenger can hope for better publicity. I like Hamburg's idea of superimposing their all-night bus routes on the picture of a dusky nude!

Finally the local government re-organisation. At the time of writing much is shrouded in mystery. PTEs will be enlarged and two more formed in this area (South Yorkshire and West Yorkshire) while a part of the Midland Red undertaking has been acquired by the West Midlands PTE. PTEs are capable of experimentation and planning far beyond the means of small operators so the future must be hopeful for the passenger. However with ever larger and ever fewer undertakings running an ever diminishing variety of vehicles the outlook for enthusiasts is regrettably bleak.

Left: Old buses will no doubt continue to form the basis of many auxiliary vehicles. Obviously going nowhere in a hurry was this Sheffield 1937 Leyland TD5c with locally-built Cravens bodywork not quite in use as an instruction bus in March, 1957

Right: Although a Midland Red subsidiary, Stratford Blue never standardised on its vehicles for the running fleet. However this ex-BMMO SON did become the Stratford Blue tree-lopper as seen under the weeping willows in August, 1960

The largest independent operator in the country, Lancashire United, seems likely to be absorbed into SELNEC in the near future. A memory of past variety is this 1949 Dennis Lance/ Weymann on the forecourt of Atherton garage in July, 1963

The National Bus Company looks to the Leyland National for its future single-deck requirements. A Midland Red example is seen at Meriden, the very centre of England, in December, 1972. Revolutionary vehicles are nothing new to the Red!

Rationalisation of NBC companies and their operating areas seems likely to continue. This Crosville 1960 Leyland Tiger Cub/ Metro-Cammell in Aberayron during September, 1972 is still in the livery of Western Welsh from whom it had recently been acquired along with its services in the area. How old-fashioned the Tiger Cub now looks compared with the Leyland National

A prewar Nottingham Regal at Parliament St depot in May, 1963 before going out to relieve the parched throats of corporation bus crews

The future of our municipal bus undertakings may be uncertain but merging with other operators is nothing new. Haslingden and Rawtenstall amalgamated some years ago—this TD5 of the former came complete with Leyland's own bodywork which was not only good looking but durable. It comes as little surprise to find Haslingden 21 looking much the same in July, 1960 as it did when new in 1938

Grimsby and Cleethorpes merged in January, 1957. This 1950 BUT of Cleethorpes was one of four with Northern Coachbuilders bodies that bore a strong resemblance to ECW practice. All four were sold to Walsall after the system closed; No59 here was the only one that was not extensively reconstructed during its spell at Walsall and is now preserved

Whatever the fate of other municipal bus undertakings, the future of Luton's whose all-Crossleys are seen here has already been decided. Luton's services are now operated by United Counties

To finish on a note of sheer nostalgia, two memories of important municipalities which are to be swallowed up by new PTEs. The AEC Regent/Roe combination has been associated with Leeds City Transport for over forty years. Here a petrol Regent reminds us of earlier days as it travels along The Headrow in 1932

Sheffield is associated with variety. This 1952 Leyland PD2/12 was one of two with rare Mann Egerton bodywork as seen in June, 1962